HOCKEY
WHO DOES WHAT?

BY RYAN NAGELHOUT

 Gareth Stevens
PUBLISHING

Please visit our website, www.garethstevens.com. For a free color catalog of all our high-quality books, call toll free 1-800-542-2595 or fax 1-877-542-2596.

Cataloging-in-Publication Data

Names: Nagelhout, Ryan.
Title: Hockey: who does what? / Ryan Nagelhout.
Description: New York : Gareth Stevens Publishing, 2018. | Series: Sports: what's your position? | Includes index.
Identifiers: ISBN 9781538204290 (pbk.) | ISBN 9781538204313 (library bound) | ISBN 9781538204306 (6 pack)
Subjects: LCSH: Hockey–Juvenile literature.
Classification: LCC GV847.25 N34 2018 | DDC 796.962–dc23

First Edition

Published in 2018 by
Gareth Stevens Publishing
111 East 14th Street, Suite 349
New York, NY 10003

Copyright © 2018 Gareth Stevens Publishing

Designer: Sarah Liddell
Editor: Ryan Nagelhout

Photo credits: Cover, p. 1 dotshock/Shuttestock.com; jersey texture used throughout Al Sermeno Photography/Shutterstock.com; chalkboard texture used throughout Maridav/Shutterstock.com; p. 5 Michael Chamberlin/Shutterstock.com; p. 6 Shooter Bob Square Lenses/Shutterstock.com; p. 7 Jonah_H/Shutterstock.com; p. 8 Domenic Gareri/Shutterstock.com; pp. 9, 28 Click Images/Shutterstock.com; p. 11 Len Redkoles/Contributor/National Hockey League/Getty Images; p. 12 Doug Pensinger/Staff/Getty Images Sport/Getty Images; p. 13 Maddie Meyer/Staff/Getty Images Sport/Getty Images; p. 15 Minas Panagiotakis/Stringer/Getty Images Sport/Getty Images; p. 16 Mitrofanov Alexander/Shutterstock.com; p. 17 Anton Gvozdikov/Shutterstock.com; p. 19 Jeff Vinnick/Stringer/Getty Images Sport/Getty Images; p. 21 Vanessa Belfiore/Shutterstock.com; p. 23 Harry How/Staff/Getty Images Sport/Getty Images; p. 25 Frederick Breedon/Stringer/Getty Images Sport/Getty Images; p. 26 Hero Images/Stone/Getty Images; p. 27 Icon Sports Wire/Contributor/Icon Sportswire/Getty Images; p. 29 Portland Press Herald/Contributor/Portland Press Herald/Getty Images.

Printed in the United States of America

CPSIA compliance information: Batch #CS17GS: For further information contact Gareth Stevens, New York, New York at 1-800-542-2595.

CONTENTS

Hit the Ice 4

Stop the Puck 6

B-E Aggressive 10

Keep It Out. 12

Stay or Skate 14

Up the Ice 16

Front and Center 18

On the Right. 20

Sniping from the Left 22

Get Back! 24

Power Plays 26

More to Learn 28

Glossary. 30

For More Information 31

Index 32

Words in the glossary appear in **bold** type the first time they are used in the text.

HIT THE ICE

Hockey might seem like a simple sport: put the puck in the net and score goals. But there's a lot more to it than that. There are six different positions in hockey, and each one has a lot of different jobs it must do on the ice.

Think of it this way—goaltenders and defensemen are both trying to stop the other team from scoring, but they each do this their own special way! There are lots of questions you might ask about the positions in hockey. What should forwards do on a **penalty** kill? And why would a goaltender leave the ice and leave the net empty? Let's find out!

STAYING SAFE

One thing every hockey player knows is that you have to play safely. If you're going to take the ice or play in your driveway, make sure you use the right safety **equipment**. Knowing the right way to play and having the right gear can keep you playing longer and make sure you have more fun!

STOP THE PUCK

The goaltender, or goalie, is the most important position in hockey. Goalies stand in front of the net in an area called the crease. The crease is usually marked with blue, and other players are supposed to stay out. Goaltenders stop shots on net taken by the other team.

It's not easy—pro players can shoot pucks more than 100 miles (160 km) per hour at the net from up close! Taking a shot to the chest isn't so bad, but stopping a hard rubber puck with your head can hurt! It can be dangerous to play goal!

PADS AND STICKS

To stay safe, goaltenders wear certain equipment on their body. They wear a special helmet, a chest protector, and long pads on their legs to stop hard shots. They wear a glove on one hand and a blocker on the hand they use to hold their stick, too.

A GOALTENDER'S STICK IS FLATTER THAN A STICK A FORWARD OR DEFENSEMAN WOULD USE. THAT'S BECAUSE IT'S USED TO STOP THE PUCK, NOT SHOOT IT!

GOALIE EQUIPMENT

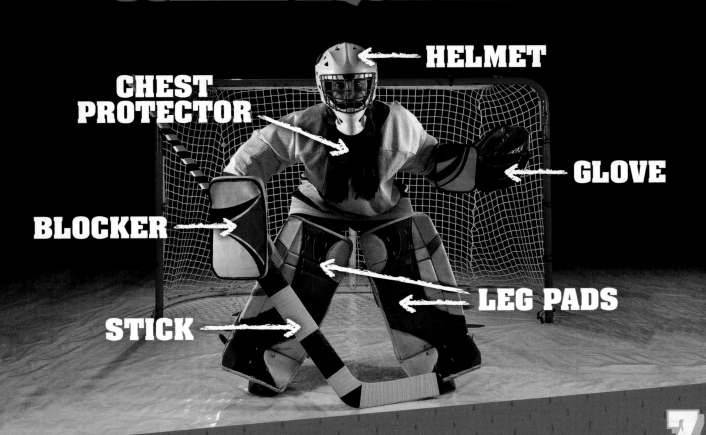

HELMET

CHEST PROTECTOR

GLOVE

BLOCKER

LEG PADS

STICK

Stopping the puck isn't as easy as standing in front of the net. Teams will try to pass the puck to move a goaltender out of position.

There are different ways goaltenders play. Today, most use the butterfly position. When someone takes a shot on net, they fall down on their knees with their legs bent and their feet facing the posts. This makes their legs look a bit like butterfly wings. With their pads pushed together, the entire bottom half of the net is blocked by the goaltender. They just have to stop higher shots with their glove, blocker, and helmet!

STILL ON SKATES

Goaltenders need quick **reflexes** to move fast and stop pucks. They also need to be strong skaters. Goalies balance on skates like other players and need to move up and down off skates quickly to make saves and move across the crease. It takes a lot of practice to get it right.

YEARS AGO, GOALTENDERS WOULD ALWAYS STAY ON THEIR FEET TO MAKE SAVES. THE BUTTERFLY POSITION CHANGED THE WAY THE GAME WAS PLAYED!

B-E AGGRESSIVE

Goaltenders can't sit back in their net all the time. They need to be **aggressive**! Goaltenders need to make themselves seem to take up more of the net to shooters by cutting down the shooter's angle on net. To do this, they move away from the net toward the person with the puck. This is called challenging the shooter.

Goalies follow the puck and keep their body in front of it. They **adjust** their position in the crease to stay "square" to the shooter, while the opposing team moves the puck around to try getting the goaltender out of position to score!

KEEP IT TOGETHER

Goalies need to be mentally tough. Sometimes they will let in a goal they should have stopped, but they can't get down on themselves! Their team depends on them to come back strong and not second-guess themselves. For a goaltender, the

KEEP IT OUT

The players on the ice who aren't goaltenders are called skaters. Each team has five skaters on the ice—three forwards and two defensemen. The two players on defense, sometimes called defenders, mostly play in the same end as their team's goaltender. Their job is to keep the other team from getting shots on goal and take the puck away from their **opponent** so their team can score goals.

There are two main kinds of defensemen—right and left. Defensemen often pick a side based on how they shoot. Left-handed shooters play on the left and right-handed shooters play on the right.

Defensemen and forwards play together in groups. Right and left defensemen playing together are called a pair. They take the ice at the same time and play a period of time called a shift. When they're tired, they hop off the ice and another pair comes on.

PICKING A SIDE BASED ON HOW YOU SHOOT LETS YOU DIG PUCKS OUT ALONG THE WALL AND COVER SPEEDY WINGERS TRYING TO GET PAST YOU ON THE SIDE.

STAY OR SKATE

Defensemen play hockey differently based on the skills they have. Big, strong defensemen often stay "at home" in the defensive zone and protect the net. They lean on the other team's offensive, or shooting, players and keep them from the net, laying hard hits on them and making scoring tough.

Offensive defensemen play more aggressively, using their skating and puck-handling abilities to join the offense and try to score. They're sometimes called puck-carrying defensemen because they bring the puck into the offensive zone, then pass to offensive players. These players need to be fast to get back on defense in case they lose the puck.

ON THE BLUE LINE

When on offensive, defensemen play near the blue line, which marks the end of the team's offensive zone. They keep the puck in their zone and pass to other players or shoot from "the point" on net. Sometimes a defender will "pinch" and go deeper into the zone to keep the other team from getting the puck outside the zone.

LOSING THE PUCK IS CALLED A TURNOVER. THE OTHER TEAM OFTEN GETS A SCORING CHANCE OFF A TURNOVER BECAUSE PLAYERS ON DEFENSE ARE OUT OF POSITION.

P.K. SUBBAN

UP THE ICE

While some defensemen are good at scoring, forwards do most of the work to put the puck in the net. There are three different kinds of forwards—centers, left wingers, and right wingers. Centers mostly play in the middle of the ice, while left and right wingers play the left and right sides of the ice.

Like defensive pairs, forwards play together on what's called a line. Each line has one center, left winger, and right winger. Pro teams have four lines. The top line often has the team's best players on it. A coach decides which players will skate together on a line.

CHANGE IT UP

Hockey is a fast game. Players skate as hard as they can, then get off the ice when they're tired. Sometimes a coach will ask an entire line to come off. Other times, a single player will get off the ice on a change because their teammates have the puck or are playing defense in their own end.

PLAYERS ON THE BENCH WAIT FOR THEIR CHANCE TO HOP ON THE ICE AND PLAY. A LINE CHANGE NEEDS TO HAPPEN FAST!

FRONT AND CENTER

The center is the most important forward position. They take all the team's face-offs, which are those times when the puck is dropped by an official to start play. Centers need quick reflexes to win face-offs by getting their stick on the puck and knocking it back to a teammate.

Winning face-offs gives a center's team possession of the puck, which is important in getting off shots and scoring goals. Face-off wins in the offensive zone are big! A team can take a quick shot right off a "clean" face-off win, or a face-off win where the puck goes right to a teammate.

LIKE A QUARTERBACK

In some ways, centers are like a football quarterback on a hockey team! They have to be smart players who work on both ends of the ice to control play. They need to lead their teammates to move the puck up ice and get others in position to score goals.

ON THE RIGHT

A right winger plays on the right side of the ice. Right wingers are usually bigger players because they work along the boards. They must play against their opponent's left defenseman, who wants to take the puck away from them. Right wingers are often right-handed, which helps them dig the puck out along the boards and make passes to the center and left winger.

Right wingers also need to be fast skaters and have quick hands so they can handle the puck. They have to be ready to take passes from the center and get **accurate** shots off from the right side of the ice.

DEFEND THE END

In the defensive end, wingers must play against the other team's defensemen. They try to block shots defensemen make from the point that cause turnovers, which can lead to scoring chances for the opposing team. A quick winger blocking a shot and getting past the other team's defense can get a shot alone on the goaltender—that's a breakaway!

SNIPING FROM THE LEFT

Left wingers are often left-handed and do many of the things right wingers do on their own side of the ice. Players on the left wing often have a good angle to shoot the puck from. Many can "snipe," or pick corners of the net to shoot at that goaltenders have trouble defending.

Wingers need to be able to get off many different kinds of shots, too. Players with more time to shoot, for example, use a hard shot with a windup called a slap shot. But wingers take quick shots called wrist or snap shots, too. They can also use the back of their stick to get shots on net called backhands.

MIX IT UP

When a team "cycles" the puck, they move it between players in the offensive zone by skating in circles around the net. This often means that players move out of position as well. The same thing happens on defense. While players often guard their parts of the ice, they can switch and cover different areas if needed.

THOUGH A POSITION IN HOCKEY COMES WITH CERTAIN RESPONSIBILITIES, IT CAN QUICKLY CHANGE IN A GAME BASED ON WHAT'S HAPPENING ON THE ICE. TEAMMATES HAVE TO COVER FOR ONE ANOTHER!

GET BACK!

Forwards aren't all about scoring goals. They have important roles on defense, too. If a player turns the puck over to the other team, they need to quickly get back on defense. If not enough players are back on defense, the opposition could have an "odd-man rush," which means they have more attacking players than the other team can defend.

When this happens, players need to skate back hard and try to get the puck back. This is called backchecking. If a team can backcheck and get the puck back, they might have an odd-man rush for themselves!

TAKE THE PASS

Defensemen work closely with goaltenders to make smart plays in hockey. If they're defending a 2-on-1 odd-man rush, for example, the goaltender follows the opposing player with the puck—that's the shooter. The defender needs to not play the shooter, but the other player so they can't get a pass from the puck carrier and get a scoring chance. They have to trust the goalie can make a save!

ODD-MAN RUSHES CREATE AN EXCITING GAME, BUT COACHES WON'T LIKE THEIR TEAM MAKING MISTAKES AND TURNING THE PUCK OVER LIKE THAT!

POWER PLAYS

When a team takes a penalty, a player goes to the penalty box. That team has to play with one less skater on the ice. The penalized team is shorthanded and must run time off the clock until the penalty is over. They almost always put a center, winger, and two defensemen on the ice on a penalty kill.

The team with the man advantage, also called a power play, puts its best players on the ice to score. Sometimes they play four forwards—one in a defenseman's spot—to get more offensive-minded players on the ice and move the puck better. Teams on the penalty kill play with two forwards and two defensemen. Some teams will even play five forwards, but two players need to play defense if they turn the puck over!

MAKE A BOX

It's hard to stop a team from scoring on a power play! Teams killing penalties set up in a box in front of their net. They try to stop passes from getting through the box and move opposing players out from in front of the net. On a 5-on-3 power play, defenders make a triangle in front of the net with their three players.

A DEFENSEMAN OFTEN LINES UP AS A WINGER ON A SHORTHANDED FACE-OFF. IF A TEAM IS TWO MEN SHORT, THEY OFTEN ONLY HAVE ONE WINGER, A CENTER, AND ONE DEFENDER!

MORE TO LEARN

Now that you've got the basics of hockey's positions down, let's learn some more advanced rules. Did you know teams can play with six skaters? If a goaltender leaves the ice, another forward can come off the bench. Teams often do this when they're losing late in a game and need to score a goal. If the other team gets the puck, though, they can score an empty-net goal.

Goaltenders will also leave the net on a delayed penalty call because when the penalized team touches the puck, the whistle is blown and the power play starts! It's like a mini-power play before the power play!

There's so much more to learn about hockey. Keep watching and playing to pick up new skills and be the best position player you can be!

LISTEN TO COACH

One important part of a team is the coach. It's important to listen to coaches who can help you learn more about your position and how to play better. They will also tell you when to change lines and tell when a goaltender should come off the ice for an extra attacker.

COACHES WANT TO HELP YOU GET BETTER AND LEARN YOUR POSITION. THE BETTER YOU PLAY, THE BETTER THE TEAM PLAYS!

GLOSSARY

accurate: free from mistakes; able to hit the target

adjust: to fix something based on new information

aggressive: showing a readiness to attack

equipment: the tools needed for a certain purpose

opponent: the person or team you must beat to win a game

penalty: loss or harm caused because of a broken rule

reflexes: the ability to react quickly

toughness: the ability to keep working and focus on a task

FOR MORE INFORMATION

BOOKS

Derr, Aaron. *Hockey: An Introduction to Being a Good Sport.* Egremont, MA: Red Chair Press, 2017.

Kortemeier, Todd. *Pro Hockey by the Numbers.* North Mankato, MN: Capstone Press, 2016.

Omoth, Tyler. *First Source to Hockey: Rules, Equipment, and Key Playing Tips.* North Mankato, MN: Capstone Press, 2016.

WEBSITES

Hockey 101: Playing the Game
sportsnet.ca/hockey/hockey-101-playing-the-game/
Learn more about hockey and how to play the game.

Hockey Positions
bluejackets.ice.nhl.com/club/page.htm?id=48215
Learn more about hockey positions from an NHL team.

The Role of a Winger in Hockey
howtohockey.com/the-role-of-a-winger-in-hockey/
Learn more about what wingers do in hockey.

INDEX

butterfly position 8, 9

center 16, 18, 19, 20, 26, 27

coach 29

defense 12, 14, 15, 17, 20, 22, 24, 26

defenseman 4, 7, 12, 13, 14, 16, 20, 24, 26, 27

equipment 4, 7

face-off 18, 27

forward 4, 7, 12, 13, 16, 18, 24, 26, 28

gloves 7, 8

goal 4, 10, 12, 18, 24, 28

goaltender 4, 6, 7, 8, 9, 10, 11, 12, 20, 22, 24, 28, 29

helmet 7, 8

left winger 16, 19, 20, 22,

line 16, 17, 29

mental toughness 10, 11

net 4, 6, 8, 10, 11, 14, 16, 22, 27, 28

odd-man rush 24, 25

offense 14, 21

pads 7, 8

pair 13

pass 8, 14, 19, 20, 24, 27

penalty 4, 26, 27, 28

power play 26, 27, 28

right winger 16, 19, 20, 22

safety 4, 7

shooter 10, 12, 24

shots 22

skater 9, 12, 20, 26, 28

skates 9

stick 7, 18, 22